The BALL PYTHON Manual

Philippe de Vosjoli
Roger Klingenberg, D.V.M.

Tracy Barker
David Barker

Table of Contents

Introduction

The ball python is currently one of the most widely sold snakes in the pet trade. In 1991, more than 65,000 ball pythons were imported into the United States alone. Thousands more were imported into European countries, Canada, and Japan. In the past, gravid females were exported, resulting in the loss of thousands of eggs and in the health decline of the females. However, during the past two years, exporters have established programs for the captive hatching of ball python eggs. As a result, increased numbers of imported hatchlings have become available, and greater total numbers of ball pythons have been exported by the countries of origin. The ball python is the last "cheap" python in the trade; consequently, it is one of the most appealing to pet store owners, as well as to first-time snake buyers.

These snakes also have appeal for many other reasons: their form, color, and pattern are attractive in a way that is distinctively African; they do not attain a size that is a problem to maintain or that could in

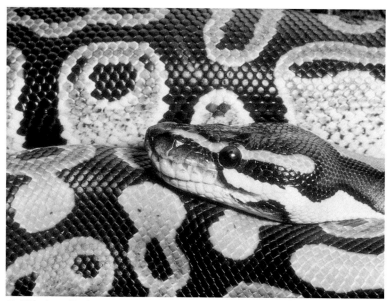

Ball Python *(Python regius). Photo by David Barker.*

any way threaten humans or most household pets; as a rule, they are reluctant to bite, and they readily become tame and are easy to handle.

On the other hand, the ball python is a highly exploited species, not only in the pet trade but also in its countries of origin, where these snakes are eaten and their skin is used as a source of leather. Unfortunately, ball pythons do not have a high reproductive rate, compared with that of some of the larger pythons. The size of their egg clutches tends to be small, and in the wild they tend to breed every two to three years, rather than every year. Careful management, including captive incubation of eggs laid by collected females and restocking programs, will be required if the current level of marketing for the pet trade is to continue. More efforts should also be made to propagate this species in captivity. To put the ball python in an economic perspective that relates to herpetoculture, simply consider that a ball python is likely to produce fewer offspring over a two-year period than a green tree python *(Morelia viridis)*, a blood python *(Python curtus)*, or a jungle carpet python *(Morelia spilota variegata)*, all of which are currently sold at prices many times greater than those of ball pythons.

Ball pythons are currently among the most readily available and least expensive larger snakes sold in the pet trade; they are also some of the most challenging. Adults and subadults tend to harbor parasites and commonly arrive with various diseases, including stomatitis (mouthrot), respiratory disorders, and protozoan and bacterial infections. Most of these medical problems usually go unnoticed and unattended by inexperienced pet-store personnel and first-time buyers. The most prevalent complaint associated with adult ball pythons is their reluctance to feed in captivity.

The goal of this book is to provide useful up-to-date information on the husbandry and propagation of this misunderstood species, including tips on how to overcome problems related to feeding.

General Information

What's In a Name?

The scientific name of the ball python is *Python regius,* which means "royal python." This is the name by which this snake is known in Europe. It is a more appropriate name than the popular "ball python" used in the United States, which refers to this species' propensity to coil into a tight ball as a defensive behavior.

Distribution

The ball python is distributed as follows: in the grasslands of the Sudanese subprovince (west of the Nile); in Southern Sudan, in the Bahrel Ghazal and Nuba Mountains region (southern Kordofan); in West Africa from Senegal to Sierra Leone; and in the Ivory Coast and parts of Central Africa.

Origin of Imports

Virtually all ball pythons currently sold in the reptile trade are imported from Togo and Ghana.

Habitat

Ball pythons are primarily terrestrial snakes that inhabit open forests or savanna grasslands with low tree density and scattered rock outcroppings. They are not found in closed forests. They are known to colonize grasslands that are the result of heavy clearing and farming, and there are reports of people setting fire to grasslands as a method of collecting these animals.

Size

Hatchlings range from ten inches (25.4 cm) for runts to 17 inches (43.2 cm). Adults range from three to five feet (.91 to 1.27 m). There are reports of individuals in the wild reaching more than six feet (1.52 m) in length.

Growth rate

Ball pythons that are captive-raised from hatchlings will grow to more than three feet in length within three years. Under an optimal growth regimen, some ball pythons will be sexually mature by 18 months of age. More typically, captive-raised animals are sexually mature by 2 1/2 to 3 1/2 years, depending upon their dietary regimen and maintenance conditions (primarily temperature).

Longevity

Ball pythons are among the longest lived of snakes. It would be reasonable to expect lifespans of 20 to 30 years with captive-raised ball pythons. The longest-lived ball python on record is held by a specimen, purchased as a young adult male by renowned herpetologist Roger Conant, which resided in the Philadelphia Zoo from April 26, 1945, to October 7, 1992, more than 47 years. This is the longest-lived snake on record (Conant 1993).

A very large imported female ball python. Two hands should be used to provide adequate support when handling any large specimen. *Photo by Philippe de Vosjoli.*

Variation

By Tracy Barker and David Barker

It is interesting to note how many ball python fanciers describe ball pythons as pale snakes with dark markings, while others see the them as dark snakes with large pale blotches. The dark markings of most ball pythons are chocolate brown; the pale markings of the average adult ball python are medium brown; in hatchlings or juveniles the pale markings are often yellow, gold or yellowish-brown. The bellies of most ball pythons are off-white or pale gray, with some gray smudges. In recent years it has become obvious that ball pythons demonstrate considerable variation in both color and pattern.

The most commonly observed ball python pattern has a dark back and dark upper surface of the head. On each side, spaced along the length of the neck and body, are 15 to 25 large, pale, rounded blotches, usually open on the bottom, connected with and shading to the paler belly coloration. The blotches are separated by dark interspaces that connect to the dark back. Each pale lateral blotch may have one or two small dark spots in the upper portion of the blotch; some populations of ball pythons do not have these small spots at all, while in other populations there may be numerous small dark freckles in the pale lateral blotches. There is a series of longitudinally elongated oval blotches of irregular lengths down the center of the back. The posterior body and tail are dark, with a well-defined pale vertebral stripe that stops short of the tip. The end of the tail is dark with a pale tip. The sides of the head are pale, and there is a dark line, usually two scales in width, from the angle of the jaw forward through the eye to the nostril. The eyes are so darkly pigmented that the pupils may be difficult to discern from the dark irises.

The pattern of ball pythons is disruptive, meaning that the visual outline of the snake is broken up by the contrasting pattern elements. This makes more difficult ready identification by visual predators that hunt by using a search image, such as raptorial birds. There is considerable individual variation of pattern; it is likely that, like fingerprints, there are no two identical ball pythons. There probably is geographic variation of pattern and color among the different populations of ball pythons, although at this time we are unable to quantify it.

Only in recent years has the extent of the pattern and color variations of ball pythons come to the attention of python fanciers. Once considered to be a fairly simple and plain little python, some of the variations of ball pythons are truly spectacular. At this time it is not known whether most of the observed color and pattern variations are inheritable as simple recessive mutations. However, many of the leading python herpetoculturists are now working with large groups of ball pythons, beginning the breeding experiments necessary to learn the genetics and inheritance of many of the pattern and color variations.

The following is a listing of many of the unusual color and pattern variations of ball pythons that are occasionally available in the herpetocultural trade. We have placed in quotations the names for particular appearances that we think are likely nebulous distinctions of normal variation.

"Yellow/yellow-orange": Youngsters are typically brighter and more yellow in coloration than adults. Most often this is a particularly attractive hatchling or juvenile that will become a normal adult. Some specimens have a distinct orange or coral wash of color along the lower margin of the sides; this color typically fades to brown as the animal matures. One interesting question regarding this form will soon be answered through selective captive breeding: will the offspring of normal adults that both had this appearance as hatchlings inherit this appearance?

"High gold": This is typically an extreme variation of the yellow phase; high-gold specimens are invariably youngsters that will become brown adults. The dark pattern is often black. Also associated with this form, accentuating the overall yellow appearance, many specimens have reduced amounts of dark pattern, and the pale blotches of the sides may cross over the back, creating the appearance of a yellow snake with dark cigar-band-shaped bands across the body.

"Jungle": This is one of the most breathtakingly beautiful of the ball pythons. Jungle ball pythons have pale yellow eyes, a pale brown spot on the top of the head, and an irregular black pattern. Hatchlings have the most vivid yellow-gold coloration of any ball python. This bright color darkens with age, and adults are brown with irregular black markings and pale eyes. It is not known whether this condition is inheritable; nevertheless, jungle ball pythons are in great demand and, when available, command high prices.

Black or melanistic: These specimens have dark pigment suffused throughout the pale areas of the pattern at all ages. Even the belly is darker. Some specimens may be so dark as to appear nearly black, although on close examination a pattern is always visible. It is our observation that black ball python hatchlings are smaller than hatchlings of other color phases. A wild-caught gravid black female laid three eggs, from which hatched three normally colored and patterned hatchlings. It has not been demonstrated through captive breeding whether or not this color-phase is inheritable as a simple recessive trait.

Axanthic: The name refers to the fact that these specimens are lacking yellow pigment. There are two conditions of axanthic ball pythons. In the typical condition, the pattern of hatchlings and adults is composed of pale gray and black markings. Someday this mutation and the albino mutation will be combined to produce a "snow" ball.

In a second, less-common condition, the normal pattern of hatchlings is composed of ivory-white and black markings. As these animals mature, increasing melanin is deposited in the white pattern area, and these animals turn increasingly dark with age, the pale areas of pattern eventually becoming dark charcoal gray, with the pattern only faintly visible. This second type of axanthic condition is termed "black and white."

Although not yet proven, it is likely that both of these axanthic conditions are inheritable as simple recessive mutations.

Xanthic: This is the opposite of the previous condition, and ball pythons with this condition are beautiful yellow or gold at all ages. It is not clear whether this condition is a result of too much yellow pigment (a true xanthic condition), or of unusually small amounts of black pigment (a condition known as hypomelanism). The dark markings of most xanthic specimens, especially the upper surface of the head, have a distinctly yellowish or greenish tinge. This is a rare condition; we are aware of only eight specimens. There may be different types and genetic bases for the xanthic condition in ball pythons; the Ugandan specimen illustrated in Pittman (1974) appears somewhat different from the xanthic specimens from Ghana. It seems highly likely that the xanthic condition is inheritable as a simple recessive trait.

Albino: This refers to the condition of amelanism, the absence of black pigment. Albino ball pythons are white snakes with yellow markings and pink or orange-pink eyes. This is a simple recessive mutation. One or two albino ball pythons are collected or hatched from wild-bred eggs each year in Ghana.

Leucistic: This is the condition of absolute white coloration, no pattern, and dark eyes. We know of only two examples of this condition, and both specimens died soon after hatching.

Piebald: The head and anterior neck of piebald ball pythons is normal in appearance and color. However, large areas of the body are milk white and patternless. Areas of normal pigmentation may occur as patches or areas along the length of the body; typically the pattern in these pigmented areas appears anomalous, often as paired, elongated dark dorsal blotches on the normal brown pigmentation. Piebald ball pythons are one of the most visually interesting and beautiful snakes in the world. The genetic basis and inheritance of this condition is not known.

"Crossover" or "banded": This is the pattern condition in which the pale blotches on each side join across the back to create the overall appearance of a pale snake with irregular dark bands. This is purported to be a geographic pattern variation common in Nigeria; it is rarely seen in specimens from populations from Ghana and Togo. Undoubtedly there is a genetic basis for this pattern, but it is likely a polygenetic character and not due to a single gene.

Striped: There are a variety of striped conditions in ball pythons. The most common striped condition results from a fusion of the longitudinally-elongated vertebral blotches on an otherwise normally patterned snake; this is apparently a random variation and is not inherited as a simple recessive trait. In a further variation known as the "wide-stripe" ball python, the pale vertebral stripe is usually 3–5 scale rows in width, perhaps 7–12 scale rows wide. One rare variation, termed a "90-degree pattern shift," is an animal with a well-defined, smooth-edged, black margined, wide pale vertebral stripe. The only such animal, in the collection of Bob Clark, has lateral pale stripes.

Another striped variation is the black-backed or black-striped ball python. This variation is characterized by the absence of the pale vertebral blotches.

Clown: The only known specimen of clown ball python is an extreme variety of black-backed ball python. This specimen has very little pattern on the sides, and an unusual pale head marked with thin dark lines. The scales around the eyes are black and one eye has a single black spot below it, a "clown tear" that is the basis for the name. The genetic basis and inheritance of the appearance of this very unusual ball python is not known.

Ghost: The ghost phase, a rare condition of ball pythons, appears to be created by unusual small rounded dorsal scales. Ghost ball pythons have an satiny iridescence not typical of ball pythons; the pattern is normal but the colors appear soft and muted. The variation is known from two wild specimens from Ghana; ghost ball pythons have not been bred in captivity.

The ball python is certainly one of the most promising snakes in herpetoculture, with many qualities that make it desirable to both breeders and fanciers. Most individuals are docile and easily handled, easy to feed and have minimal space requirements for a python. Ball pythons have a low reproductive rate, which, from a commercial point of view, means that many of the lineages of spectacular color and pattern that prove to be inheritable will remain rare and valuable for many years to come. The great variations of color and pattern just discussed give serious ball python breeders opportunities for selective breeding unequalled in any other python species. We can look forward to more beautiful domestic lineages of extraordinary color and pattern in the years to come.

Selection

Before Buying a Ball Python

An adult *imported* specimen of the ball python is not a good beginner's snake. If you are purchasing your first snake, you would probably do better to choose one of the many captive-bred colubrids (such as a corn snake or kingsnake), or one of the boas or other pythons. On the other hand, captive-hatched ball pythons, usually available in spring and summer, are good choices for herpetoculturists wishing to work with this species. The spotted python *(Antaresia maculosa)*, now captive-bred in the United States, is another good choice as a beginner's python that remains small.

The reason that the ball python is not a good choice for beginners (unless purchased as a hatchling or as a juvenile) is that imported adults tend to be difficult to acclimate and to start feeding. They also commonly harbor parasites that should be treated. Most beginning hobbyists become discouraged during the task of persuading imported adult ball pythons to feed. They may also become discouraged during the course of parasite treatment and possibly (if not enough care was given to initial selection) with the problems associated with the treatment of respiratory disorders, stomatitis (mouthrot), and enteric diseases (all too common in imported animals).

> Success with ball pythons will, to a significant degree, depend upon the initial selection of a potentially healthy animal. Because many diseases and disorders cannot be determined by visual or tactile inspection, it is not possible to positively ascertain the health of an animal without veterinary assistance.

Selecting a Potentially Healthy Ball Python

The following are guidelines for evaluating the health of ball pythons. They will help you select a potentially healthy snake, one that has a good chance of acclimating to captivity.

First, prior to requesting that a specific animal be handed over to you for inspection, select one of the smaller (and thus younger) animals, one that has a rounded body and that does not demonstrate pronounced backbone or rib definition. The best ball pythons to start with are captive-hatched juveniles, and imported juveniles are a close second. Check to be sure that the skin is relatively clear and free of superficial injuries.

Second, ask that the animal be handed to you. Once in hand, a healthy ball python should give a distinct impression of strength and good muscle tone. Newly imported ball pythons in good health also usually have a strong tendency to adopt the tight defensive "ball" posture. Avoid animals that give an impression of limpness and/or poor muscle tone. These are *always* clear indicators of poor health.

Next, you should perform the following series of steps to determine details of health:

1. Hold the snake behind its head with one hand (while supporting the body on a table or using your arm to hold it against your body); with the other hand gently pull the skin underneath the lower jaw to open the mouth of the animal. Look for the presence of bubbly mucus which is a sign of respiratory infection. Another technique (although not as reliable) to determine this is to leave the mouth of the snake closed, and with the thumb of your free hand, gently press up against the throat area. If a snake has a respiratory infection, this will often cause mucus to emerge from the sides of the mouth or through the nostrils. Avoid any snake with signs of respiratory infection.

2. While you have the animal's mouth open, look for signs of mouthrot (stomatitis). When it is present, areas of the gums will be covered with caseous (cheesy-looking) matter. In some cases, red, raw, and injured areas will be evident. Avoid any animals with these symptoms.

3. While you have the animal in hand, also check the eyes to be sure that they are clear. If the snake is in shed, both eyes should demonstrate equal levels of opacity (clouding over).

4. Check the body for lumps. Check also for depressed areas along the backbone and for collapsed areas along the sides of the body, a sign of broken ribs. Avoid snakes with any of these symptoms.

5. Examine the belly area to be sure it is free of signs of infection, including raised ventral scales, stained scales and/or damaged scales.

When buying a ball python, the best choice is a captive-born hatchling.
Photo by Philippe de Vosjoli.

6. Examine the vent (opening to the cloaca) to be sure that the anal
scale lies flat against the body and is free of any caked or crusty
matter. Be sure that the surrounding area is free of signs of smeared
diarrhea. *Avoid snakes with these symptoms.*

7. Look for ticks. These are large, rounded and flat external parasites, harbored by virtually all imported ball pythons. If they are
present, simply keep in mind that they will have to be removed when
the animal gets home. Next check the animal for mites. These are
tiny, rounded, beadlike arthropods that usually can be seen moving
on the body; they also can be seen imbedded between the rim of the
eye and the eye itself, giving a raised impression to the eye rim. Two
reliable indicators of mites are the presence of scattered white flecks
(mite feces) on the body of a snake and, following inspection of a
snake, the presence of tiny mites crawling on your hands. Unless you
are willing to deal with the treatment of these parasites, avoid mite-
infested snakes. If you have other snakes in your collection, it is
generally not a good idea to purchase snakes with these parasites. Be
sure to wash your hands after handling the snake.

Acclimation

Quarantine

If you are keeping other reptiles (including other ball pythons), you should quarantine any newly purchased ball pythons and keep them in individual enclosures in a room or building other than where you currently maintain your collection. This procedure is recommended to prevent the introduction and spread of diseases in an established collection. Standard protocol is to quarantine any newly obtained animal for 60 to 90 days prior to introducing them into any enclosure or room where established specimens are maintained.

Steps in Acclimating Ball Pythons

1. If you are serious about owning a ball python, you should contact a good reptile veterinarian and have him or her conduct a stool check for parasites. All imported ball pythons tend to be infected with a number of parasites, which should be treated. These parasites may include pentastomes, roundworms (nematodes), flukes (trematodes),

Once acclimated and feeding regularly, ball pythons can occasionally be handled for brief periods of time. *Photo by Philippe de Vosjoli.*

and tapeworms (cestodes), as well as protozoans such as *Giardia, Trichomonas, Entamoeba,* and coccidia. Ball pythons that have been treated for parasites are more likely to acclimate than those left untreated. Considering the current low price of ball pythons, the expense of veterinary treatment of parasites should be affordable to most buyers. If you cannot afford the cost of treatment, then you should probably purchase a captive-bred ball python rather than an imported specimen.

2. First, remove any ticks by using a cotton swab to apply rubbing alcohol to the body of the tick. Wait a few minutes and then pull out the imbedded tick with a pair of tweezers.

3. Place the ball python in a suitable enclosure on newspaper (see chapter on *Housing and Maintenance*), with heat gradients, including an area reaching a surface temperature of 90–95°F (32.2–35° C), a shelter, and a large water bowl filled with clean fresh water (repeat once a week or whenever it is fouled). Leave the animal alone for two weeks; do not handle it except to administer parasite treatment or to clean the cage (which will probably not be necessary during the first week). Check for mites, which may only become apparent at a later time, and proceed with treatment if it becomes necessary.

4. After the initial two-week settling-in period, and assuming that the snake is not ready to go into shed (signaled by the dull appearance of the skin and clouding of the eyes), proceed with the feeding steps indicated in the section called *Feeding.*

Ball pythons require several weeks, even months in some cases, to acclimate to captivity. Once acclimated, animals will feed with some regularity and thus gain and maintain weight. In time, they will tolerate varying amounts of handling.

Housing and Maintenance

Selecting an Enclosure

Ball pythons should be kept in enclosures that are specially constructed to house snakes securely. These include commercial, all-glass enclosures with sliding-screen tops, commercial fiberglass enclosures with sliding-glass fronts, and custom-built wood or melamine-coated wood enclosures with front-opening framed glass or plexiglass doors. Cages that are not specifically constructed for housing snakes, such as all-glass aquaria with screened lids (usually sold for housing small mammals), are *not* escape-proof. Always keep in mind that ball pythons are powerful and notorious escape artists. Be a responsible herpetoculturist; buy the proper type of enclosure or have one built. If you are using a hinged lid or door rather than a sliding top or front, be sure that the lid or door has a secure locking mechanism that will prevent a snake from escaping.

A basic ball python setup using a commercial all-glass vivarium with sliding-screen top and locking pin. *Photo by Philippe de Vosjoli.*

Size of Enclosure

The minimum enclosure for housing a juvenile ball python should have a floor surface area at least as large as that of a standard ten-gallon aquarium (20 inches long by 10 inches wide or 50.8 cm long by 25.4 cm wide). For small adults, the enclosure should have a floor area of a standard 20-gallon aquarium (24 inches long by 12 inches wide or 61 cm long by 30.5 cm wide); a larger size is preferable. For very large adults, an enclosure with a floor area of at least a standard 30-gallon aquarium (36 inches long by 12 inches wide or 91.4 cm long by 30.5 cm wide) should be considered.

Every time a snake escapes, it provides fuel for the arguments of those who want to ban the ownership of exotic animals, including reptiles. Besides, members of the general public have a right to live without the unexpected visit of an escaped snake in their yard or their home. Please be a responsible snake owner for all our sakes.

This 36-inch commercial snake enclosure by Neodesha Plastics (Neodesha, Kansas) is ideal for keeping a single ball python. Heating and lighting systems are also available. *Courtesy of Neodesha Plastics.*

Substrates

Until a ball python is acclimated, the best substrate is newspaper or newsprint. The use of this substrate allows you to clean the cage easily and to readily monitor the condition of the feces and other aspects of maintenance (for example, the possible presence of mites). If mites are present, newspaper can be removed easily, thus providing the bare enclosure that is required for effective treatment.

Once the animal is acclimated, you can use a more decorative substrate. These include shredded cypress bark, pine shavings, aspen shavings, or medium-grade orchid bark (fir bark chips). You should take special precautions when using pine shavings. First, be sure that no cedar shavings, which are toxic to snakes, are mixed in; second, avoid pine shavings with a strong pine scent, as they are high in phenols and not recommended for use with snakes. When using aspen shavings, apply a thick layer and allow the snake time to compress the shavings before feeding it. If you use either pine or aspen shavings, it is highly recommended that you inspect the snake's mouth area regularly to make sure that shavings have not become lodged in its mouth.

Heating

Ball pythons require relatively high temperatures to fare well in captivity. In your snake's enclosure, the ambient daytime temperature should be 80–85° F (26.7–29.4° C). Also establish a temperature gradient to allow the snake to thermoregulate. You can accomplish this by creating a warmer basking area, which should reach 90–95° F (32.2–35° C) over one-fourth to one-third of the total surface area of the enclosure. It is critical that ball pythons also have access to cooler ambient temperatures. At night the ambient temperature can safely drop to a range of 75–80° F (23.9–26.7° C), as long as a heat source remains available for basking. During the winter, when you are conditioning the animals for breeding, the nighttime temperatures should be cooler by 5-8° F (2.7–4.4° C), dropping to 70–75° F (21.1 –23.9° C). (See section on *Reproduction in Ball Pythons*).

There are several heating systems for reptile enclosures now being sold in pet stores. The best ones for creating a basking area and a heat gradient are the various subtank heating pads and strips, such as the ones distributed by Hagen (formerly Flex Watt® heating strips, these should be used with a rheostat-type control), Ultratherm® heat strips (available with thermostatic controls), and subtank heating units by Zoo Med® and Tetra Terrafauna®. The Tropic Zone® hard plastic enclosed heaters are a favorite of many herpetoculturists; these have several safety features and generate a hot spot up to 20° F (11.1° C) above ambient air temperature.

When selecting a heating system, it is important to consider the ability it gives you to control the temperature, particularly with some of the heat strips and adhesive subtank heating pads. (Tropic Zone® heaters have features which make them relatively safe.) Without a temperature control such as a rheostat, some heaters can become burning hot to the touch. Some of them have been known to crack the bottoms of glass enclosures because of the high heat generated. In at least one case reported to the author, the pine shavings on the floor of an enclosure caught fire as a result.

A melamine-coated wood enclosure with locking-glass front, manufactured by Sandmar Enterprises (El Cajon, California). These units are available with lighting and heating systems controlled by thermostats. *Courtesy of Sandmar Enterprises.*

Another method of heating ball python enclosures is the use of red incandescent light bulbs in fixtures with aluminum reflectors (see *Lighting* below) or ceramic infrared heaters. You will need a thermometer to determine the appropriate wattage of the bulb for the space you will be heating. A thermostatic control is recommended.

"Hot rocks" are generally not recommended for ball pythons, because they tend to wrap around these heaters and burn themselves. Most commercial hot rocks are also too small and often too warm. If you need to use a hot rock, buy one with a temperature control, and adjust the surface temperature with the help of a thermometer.

> Always be alert to any factors that could cause a fire when you use or install a heating system for reptiles. Use common sense. Keep heat-generating lights and systems away from flammable materials. Use surge suppressors. Have a smoke alarm in any room that contains reptile enclosures with lighting and heating systems.

Lighting

Lighting seems to be of relatively little importance in the maintenance of ball pythons. As long as all other conditions are met, including the availability of a heat gradient, ball pythons will fare well, even if maintained under low light. Many herpetoculturists interested in breeding ball pythons manipulate the photoperiod to simulate long days during the summer months and short days during the winter months. They typically set lights (usually fluorescent lights, so that minimal amounts of radiant heat are generated) on timers so that the light is on 13 to 14 hours a day during most of the year, then reduced to 10 to 11 hours a day during the winter cooling period required for successful breeding. Whether manipulation of light plays a significant role in the breeding of species that live near the equator—and thus are exposed to more or less steady and equal daily periods of light and darkness throughout the year—is a factor which has yet to be determined.

If you use incandescent bulbs over a basking area to provide a heat gradient, you should use red incandescent bulbs—which are available in large hardware stores, in specialized lighting stores, and by mail order—rather than standard bulbs. The bulbs should be attached to incandescent fixtures with aluminum reflectors and placed outside the enclosure on or above the screen top. If you place an incandescent bulb inside an enclosure, you must enclose it within a wire mesh basket in order to prevent the possibility of thermal burns to your snake. Never place a bulb in such a manner that an animal can make direct contact with it.

With any lighting system, take every precaution to prevent the possibility of fire. Use ceramic fixtures that are designed to accommodate the wattage of the bulb you are using. Never place heat-generating incandescent bulbs near or in contact with flammable materials. This includes curtains, wood, walls, and plastic wiring. Use surge-suppressor outlets and always have a smoke detector in any room where you are keeping reptiles.

Monitoring Equipment

Thermometers

A thermometer is recommended to monitor the temperature where you keep ball pythons. Stores specializing in reptiles now sell inexpensive thermal-sensitive strips and other themometers that will work reasonably well for general purposes. For more exact readings, particularly if you are interested in breeding ball pythons, a digital-readout thermometer with an external probe is recommended. If you place it near a basking site, the probe can give you a continuous readout of the high-end temperature in your enclosure. These thermometers will also prove invaluable for monitoring incubating eggs. (Reasonably priced digital-readout thermometers can be purchased from Radio Shack® stores, among others.)

Thermostats

There are several kinds of thermostats currently marketed in the reptile trade. They provide an effective way of controlling the temperature in your ball python enclosures. A few specialized pet stores stock them, but you probably will have to order them by mail through publications such as *The Vivarium, Reptile & Amphibian Magazine,* or *Reptiles.* There are two categories of thermostats: on/off thermostats, which turn a heating system on or off to maintain the proper temperature, and pulse-proportional thermostats, which essentially dim or reduce the heat output to maintain the set temperature. The pulse-proportional thermostats allow for less temperature fluctuation than on/off thermostats and are highly recommended for incubating eggs.

Shelters

Ball pythons of all sizes should be provided with a suitable shelter that allows them seclusion from light and affords them a sense of security. Several attractive shelters, molded of plastic or concrete, are now sold in pet stores; these are suitable for ball pythons. As a temporary measure, you can use a cardboard box with a circular hole serving as an entryway for the snake. With imported ball pythons, shelters with an opening at the top are recommended until they begin feeding (see section on *Feeding*). Attractive and natural looking shelters can be made from large, curled sections of cork bark which you can obtain from specialized reptile dealers and pet stores. Remember: a shelter is a basic requirement for the successful maintenance of ball pythons.

A digital thermometer with an external probe. These are recommended for monitoring background and basking site temperatures.
Photo by Philippe de Vosjoli.

Horizontal cork shelter

Vertical cork shelter

Clay shelter

Three types of shelters which can be used with ball pythons.

Feeding

R efusal to feed is the problem most commonly associated with ball python maintenance. It is the complaint most often voiced by new ball python owners to pet store retailers. It is also the primary reason that an adult ball python is not a good beginner's snake.

The first thing to remember is that if the ball python you have selected is healthy, it will be able to fast for several months without any ill effects. Reports of ball pythons fasting for up to a year before they begin feeding are not uncommon. There are two records of ball pythons having fasted for up to 22 months. *Therefore, do not panic.*

One important consideration with an imported ball python is what it has been exposed to before you acquired it. Because of the overcrowded conditions in which ball pythons are kept at various stages of their travels from compounds in the countries of origin to animal dealers in the United States, these snakes are exposed to many parasites and diseases (often spread by infected sources of water) that will affect their health and impair their ability to fast for long periods of time. Therefore, if you are serious about wanting to keep a ball python, have it checked out by a veterinarian and treated for parasites and diseases.

Excessive Handling: A Primary Cause of Refusal to Feed in Ball Pythons

The tendency to coil demonstrated by most imported ball pythons is a sign of stress. This is a type of behavior that the animal performs when it feels threatened. Many first-time snake owners are so charmed by their ball python's docility (it coils up in a ball or moves between the handler's hands without biting) that they fail to recognize their animal is, in fact, stressed. If your new ball python is active, it is probably exhibiting flight behavior, trying to escape what it feels to be a threatening situation. If you are concerned because your ball python is not feeding, you should first realize that a stressed ball python usually will not feed; this means that if you want it to start feeding, you are going to have to stop handling it until it becomes accustomed to its captive environment. Considering the fact that most first-time ball python buyers seem to be overtaken by a handling compulsion, it would seem correct to assert that this is very probably a primary cause of ball pythons' refusal to feed and thus indirectly a primary cause of death. Therefore, *please keep your hands off your newly purchased snake and let it settle into its new environment.*

Rule #1: Hands off until a ball python has fed at least four times in a row when offered food. After a ball python appears to be feeding regularly, limit your handling to a maximum of 15 minutes per week. You can increase handling time after the snake has been feeding for three or four months. Stop handling anytime it stops feeding again.

Feeding Hatchlings and Subadults

If you have selected captive-bred or imported hatchlings of normal size, 15 inches (38.1 cm) and up, then feeding is usually no problem. Hatchlings typically feed within a couple of weeks after their first shed, which usually occurs one to two weeks after they hatch. They will normally feed readily on seven-to-ten-day old ("fuzzy") or just-weaned mice. "Runt" ball pythons can be difficult to start feeding and at first may have to be force-fed pre-killed five-day-old mice. Before resorting to force-feeding, offer food on several occasions for a period of up to four weeks after the first shed. Force-feeding is always stressful, so you should not resort to it before you have made a concerted effort to encourage a snake to feed on its own accord.

To force-feed a hatchling or juvenile ball python, gently grab the snake behind its head while keeping its body supported, either with your hand or with your arm against your body. With your other hand, using small, smooth, round-tipped forceps or straight hemo-static forceps (available through medical supply houses or special-ized reptile dealers), insert *head first* a pre-killed mouse between the jaws of the snake. Once the mouse is between the jaws, gently push with the forceps past the python's throat area. Release the mouse and gently remove the forceps. Immediately thereafter, place the hatchling back in its cage and leave the area. If left undisturbed, hatchlings will usually proceed to swallow force-fed prey inserted just past the throat.

Smaller ball pythons, those less than two feet in length, typically begin feeding within a few weeks or months on mice, fuzzy rats, or weanling gerbils offered intermittently, once or twice a week. As long as your snake's weight is adequate, there is no need to resort to force-feeding.

Feeding Schedule

Hatchling and subadult ball pythons should be offered food every 5 to 7 days; adults, every 7 to 10 days. Hatchlings should be offered one food item of suitable size (apparent body girth of prey animal nearly equal to thickest girth of the snake). Adults can be offered 2 or 3 prey items, such as adult mice or just-weaned rats, or a single larger prey, such as a small rat.

Problem Snakes

Virtually every imported adult ball python sold in the pet trade is a problem snake when it comes to feeding. You must take into account many factors when you have difficulty in persuading a ball python to start feeding. The first thing to consider is the ball python's feeding habits in the wild. Wild ball pythons are almost exclusively rodent eaters, feeding on several species of native African rodents, including various rats, gerbils, and gerboas. Wild ball pythons are primarily active at night and are considered to be active predators, investigating holes and rodent burrows for possible prey. They do not readily feed on mice or on the same species of rat that we normally offer to snakes, simply because these species are not found in their native habitats. Thus they have to be "converted" to new prey with significantly different scents before they will begin feeding in captivity.

In the wild, ball pythons do not feed during the times of the year when night temperatures drop into the low 70s° F or lower (20–22.8° C). In their native habitats, ball pythons tend to be inactive and off feed during December and January, when the sharp night temperature drops occur. Breeding usually occurs following this period, and many ball pythons may remain off feed at that time. After breeding, most females do not feed while they are gravid. After egg-laying, they brood their eggs, and they do not feed during this period either, even though it may last for three months. Therefore, ball pythons have the ability to withstand long periods of fasting without ill effects. Imported ball pythons shipped between November and April of a given year may be influenced by internal and external factors that may cause them to enter a fasting period.

Feeding Methods for Ball Pythons

It is very important to remember: *be patient* and *do not panic*. Many wild-caught ball pythons imported between November and April may not decide to feed until May or June.

Standard Method

1. Allow a newly purchased ball python to acclimate for two to four weeks.

2. Provide the ball python with a shelter. A shelter with an opening at the top (such as a large inverted clay flowerpot with an enlarged drainage hole) is recommended by herpetoculturists for use when feeding ball pythons. With this type of shelter, the ball pythons can be isolated from any prey placed in the vivarium until it decides to emerge and capture the prey. Rodents that enter a shelter through a side opening and pester a ball python can elicit a defensive response in the snake and thereby discourage feeding.

3. Make sure that the ambient temperature in the vivarium is 85° F (29.4° C), with a 90–95° F (32.2–35° C) warm area.

4. Be sure the ball python is not going into shed.

5. At night introduce two fuzzy (unweaned) rats. If this approach fails, repeat once each week at least two more times. If this fails, repeat this procedure using an adult mouse. If this fails, offer a pre-killed gerbil. (Note: avoid using live adult gerbils. These animals can be aggressive and have been known to attack snakes.) Repeat once a week for two more weeks. Switch back to a rat at least twice. Switch to pre-killed, just-weaned rats. Switch back to a pre-killed gerbil. Try a live, unweaned gerbil. Try pre-killed adult mice.

If, after trying all of the above you are still without success, try one of the following methods.

Brown-bag Method

1. Take a brown paper grocery bag; perforate it a few times with a paper punch.

2. With the ambient temperature of the vivarium at 85–90° F (29.4–32.2° C), introduce the ball python to an almost-weaned rat (with its eyes still closed) inside the bag. Fold over the top of the bag and staple it shut; leave it in the vivarium overnight. Check the next morning. If this method fails, repeat the procedure once each week for two more weeks. Then try the procedure with a barely weaned gerbil, or try a pre-killed adult gerbil. Then try the procedure with a pre-killed mouse.

3. Repeat this entire method.

Rodent-hole Method

1. Be sure to use a large vivarium.

2. At night, place a small plastic bucket, with a hole halfway up its side, in the vivarium. The hole must be just large enough to allow the snake to enter the bucket. Inside the bucket, place some shavings and litter of the rodent you are going to offer. Then add a fuzzy or nearly weaned rat. Put a lid on the bucket. Leave it overnight. If this fails, repeat once a week for at least two weeks. If this method fails, repeat this procedure using an adult mouse or a nearly weaned gerbil. If this attempt fails, repeat the procedure using a pre-killed rodent.

3. Repeat all steps of this entire method.

Leaf/grass-scent Method

1. Remove the ball python from its cage and place a layer of dry grass or leaf litter on the bottom of the enclosure.

2. Follow the preceding steps for standard method.

3. Once the ball python has started feeding, at first replace only a portion of the grass/leaf litter with your personal selection of substrate. Gradually replace the remaining grass/leaf litter with new substrate.

If all of the above methods fail, keep trying. The usual pattern is that just as you are at your wit's end, you look into the enclosure one day and the rodent is gone. You really cannot believe your eyes, so you look thoroughly all over the vivarium and then think, "Well, I'll be, how about that!" and immediately spread the news to your family and friends.

Once a ball python begins feeding on any of the aforementioned prey items, larger prey can be offered in sizes that would appear suitable for the size of your snake (for example, small weaned rats offered to adult snakes). You may also try to switch your ball python to a more readily available prey, such as small rats instead of gerbils. One method is to scent an alternative prey by maintaining it for one or two days in soiled litter from the type of prey you are currently feeding your snake. You should offer the litter-scented prey to the snake immediately upon removing it from the soiled litter.

Force-feeding

If treated for parasites and maintained under proper conditions, ball pythons that are not feeding will not lose a great deal of weight, even after as long as a year. If, however, your animal is showing a marked loss of weight, it would be wise to attempt to force-feed it before its weight loss becomes too severe. Once an animal is emaciated and weakened, the force-feeding procedure may cause enough additional stress to hasten its demise. Your snake should *never* be allowed to reach that point.

At the outset, the herpetoculturist must realize that force-feeding is a stressful process. When a healthy and underweight ball python is picked up and handled for force-feeding, its natural tendency is to struggle and coil and resist the process. Thus, force-feeding tends to elicit a defensive reaction. which in snakes also means an increased tendency to regurgitate ingested prey.

A Step-by-step Approach to Force-feeding Whole Prey

1. Pre-kill a small fuzzy rat or a small adult mouse. To accomplish this in a quick and humane way, hold the rodent by the tail and with a swift motion strike the back of its head against the edge of a table. If you are in doubt, ask that your rodent supplier do this for you. Next, lubricate the pre-killed prey with water or beaten whole egg.

2. Remove the ball python from its cage and take it to a table. Ask a friend to assist you. Next, take hold of the snake behind the head, gently yet firmly enough to hold it in hand while allowing its body to rest on the table. If you prefer, stabilize the snake's body with your arm by holding the snake against your body. If a friend is present, you may ask her or him to hold the body. With your other hand, using large, round-tipped forceps, grasp the lubricated pre-killed rodent behind the head and gently push it, head first, between the jaws of the ball python. You shouldn't have to apply much force during this process. A snake will usually begin to open its mouth under these conditions.

Push the rodent in as far as you can past the throat area. This is when a friend is helpful. Ball pythons tend to form a coil in the neck area that will resist the passage of the force-fed prey. At about one-tenth of the total length of the snake, another coil will resist the passage of the prey. When the prey is pushed in past the neck, release the rodent and gently remove the forceps. Then, using your thumb against the ventral surface, try to push the prey about one-third down the body length of the snake. Once again, do this *very* gently. Then, immediately carry the animal to its cage, release it and cover the cage so that it cannot see you or be disturbed in any way. In most cases, the snake will retain its force-fed prey. If it regurgitates, wait a couple of days and then repeat the process.

Force-feeding of any type is a procedure best performed by experienced individuals. Remember: the force-feeding process itself is stressful to snakes. During the course of the process you must use good judgment to determine the reaction of the animal being force-fed. If you are in doubt, take your snake to a qualified reptile veterinarian.

Force-feeding a Liquified Diet

A liquified diet consisting of three parts chicken baby food, one part whole egg, one-half part Pet Kalorie® or Nutrical®, and one part water, can be tube-fed. Use a large catheter tube on a syringe with a Luer tip, all of which can be purchased at a medical supply house. The tube should be lubricated prior to introduction and gently advanced down the esophagus to just beyond one-fourth of the body length.

You must use care during this procedure; it is best performed by a reptile veterinarian or an experienced herpetoculturist (see section on *Diseases and Disorders*).

It Fed!

Even after a ball python begins feeding, you can still expect periods of time when it will go off its feed. It usually takes several months before an imported adult ball python will feed on a regular schedule. It may even be necessary to repeat some of the techniques that you used to get it to start feeding. The key with the ball python is to be patient and persistent. If the snake has good body weight to begin with and has been treated for parasites, remember: *do not panic.*

Obesity

In captivity, overfeeding and lack of activity can cause ball pythons to become obese. Obesity increases their risk of disease, affects their ability to reproduce, and ultimately shortens their lives. There are three observable symptoms of obesity in snakes: stretched skin that causes exposure of skin between the scales, difficulty in forming coils, and fold lines in the skin when a fat snake remains in a coiled position for prolonged periods of time. When these symptoms are present the solution is simple: gradually cut back on the feeding schedule by decreasing the amount fed and/or feeding less frequently until the symptoms disappear, and then adjusting the feeding schedule to maintain the animal's proper weight.

Water

Ball pythons should always have available to them a container such as a medium-size dog water dish, half to three-fourths filled with clean water for drinking. Providing a larger water bowl when a snake is in shed may help facilitate shedding; at other times a smaller container is best in order to discourage excessive soaking. A water bowl placed partially over a heat source will also result in increased relative humidity within the vivarium, which may be beneficial at various times. Take care to assure that the vivarium has adequate ventilation, so that moisture does not accumulate as a result of condensation. A damp vivarium encourages the growth of molds and provides a medium conducive to the development of bacterial infections that cause skin blister disease.

A ball python *(Python regius)*, representative of a wild morph imported from Ghana/Togo. *Photo by David Barker.*

A close-up of a wild morph of the ball python. *Photo by David Barker.*

A close-up of the head of a ball python. *Photo by David Barker.*

The underside of the head of a ball python. *Photo by David Barker.*

(Right) A "high gold" ball python, an immature animal. *Photo by David Bark*

A "jungle" ball python. The pale yellow irises are a good indicator of this particular morph. *Photo by David Barker.*

Another variant of "jungle" ball python. *Photo by David Barker.*

A morph of the ball python in which the light lateral blotches are partially edged in pure white. *Photo by David Barker.*

Normal and axanthic (lacking yellow pigmentation) ball pythons. *Photo by David Barker.*

A "high gold" and an axanthic ball python. *Photo by David Barker.*

An axanthic "IMG" (increasing melanin gene) morph of the ball python. *Photo by David Barker.*

(Right) An axanthic ball python. *Photo by David Barker.*

Black or melanistic ball python. *Photo by David Barker.*

An outstanding example of a striped ball python. *Photo by David Barker.*

A wide-striped ball python. *Photo by David Barker.*

Another variation of a striped ball python. *Photo by David Barker.*

A "clown" striped ball python. In this morph, which is probably not of genetic origin, the middorsal series of light-colored blotches is absent and the light-colored lateral blotches are extended and fused, resulting in an irregular middorsal stripe. *Photo by David Barker.*

Another unusual pattern morph of the ball python. *Photo by David Barker.*

A piebald ball python. *Photo by David Barker.*

An albino ball python. *Photo by David Barker.*

A "high yellow" albino ball python. *Photo by David Barker.*

Close-up of a "high yellow" albino ball python. *Photo by David Barker.*

Ball pythons copulating. *Photo by David Barker.*

A gravid female ball python. *Photo by David Barker.*

A female ball python displaying maternal brooding of eggs. *Photo by David Barker.*

Ball python eggs hatching. *Photo by David Barker.*

(Right) A ball python hatching. Once the shell is slit, these snake should be allowed to emerge on their own. *Photo by David Barker.*

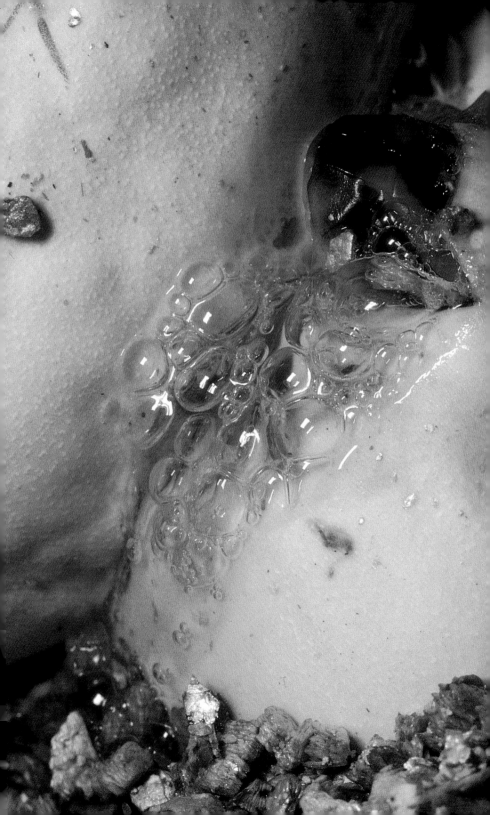

A hatchling ball python with head just emerging from shell. Note the egg tooth at the tip of the snout. *Photo by David Barker.*

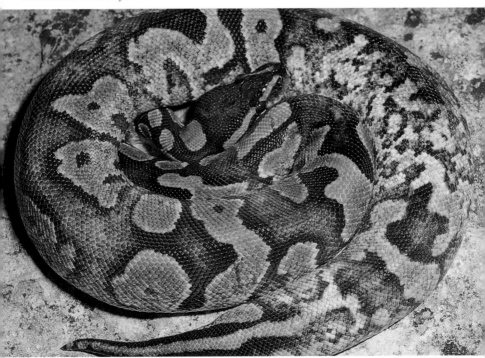

Another variant of the ball python. *Photo by David Barker.*

Handling

When you first obtain a ball python, it will readily adopt its ball-like defensive posture. Once it is in this position, you should allow the snake to remain as it is. Make no attempt to force it out of this position except for required treatment and inspection. Most imported ball pythons will perform this behavior and hide their heads rather than attempt to bite. A few specimens will be more aggressive and will adopt the coiled neck and forebody posture that precedes a strike. When a ball python does strike, it usually consists of a quick strike-bite-and-let-go sequence, resulting in multiple superficial lacerations on the area of the bite. Once acclimated, and with occasional gentle handling, most ball pythons become quite tame and less likely to adopt the characteristic defensive behavior. For obvious reasons, it is recommended that you keep ball pythons away from your face during the initial handling and taming process.

Once one is experienced, it is easy to hold a snake behind the head, moving the thumb forward and pulling down the lower "lip" to enable examination of the mouth. *Photo by Philippe de Vosjoli.*

When You Can No Longer Keep Your Ball Python

L ife is characterized by change, and in the lives of human beings change is occurring at an ever-increasing rate. Personal, financial, psychological, career-related and other circumstances may cause someone to be no longer interested in keeping, or unable to keep, a ball python (for example, your new landlord won't allow it). When faced with such situations, there are a number of recourses.

1. The first is to give your ball python and its setup to friends or relatives, along with detailed information on its care.

2. A second option is to offer your snake to a local pet store or specialized reptile dealer. Realize that if you sell the snake you will receive only one-third to one-half of its retail price. If you are desperate, be aware that few stores that sell reptiles will refuse a healthy ball python that is simply given to them.

3. Another choice is to advertise your ball python for sale, either through a classified ad in the newspaper or through herpetological society newsletters.

4. Yet another possibility is to contact a local herpetological society and inquire whether they have an adoption program.

5. As the very last resort, you can call your local animal control and inquire whether they have an adoption program for reptiles.

> Under no circumstances should you ever release a ball python. To do this could jeopardize the rights of herpetoculturists to keep snakes in a responsible manner. Never do this.

Conclusion

O nce you have resolved the initial challenges and obstacles that go with ball python ownership, this snake—because of its relatively small size, its attractive appearance, and its docile personality—ranks as one of the best pythons for herpetoculturists. With the increased interest in captive breeding, growing numbers of captive-bred hatchlings can be expected to become available in the future, including albino ball pythons and "morphs" selectively bred for outstanding color and pattern.

Source Materials

Cansdale, G.S. 1961 (reprinted 1973): *West African Snakes*. Longman Group Ltd., London. 74 pp.

Carter, R. 1990: "Captive Propagation of the Ball Python." *The Monitor*, Vol. II, #3.

Conant, R. 1993: "The Oldest Snake." *Bulletin of the Chicago Herpetological Society*. Vol. 28, #4. pp. 77-78.

Frye, F.L. 1981: *Biomedical and Surgical Aspects of Captive Reptile Husbandry*. Veterinary Medicine Publishing Co. Kansas.

Peterson, K. 19 93: "Husbandry and Breeding of Ball Pythons." *The Vivarium* (Vol.5 No.1 1993).

Pitman, C.R.S. 1974: *A Guide to the Snakes of Uganda* (Revised edition). Wheldon and Wesley, Codicote, 290 pp.

Ross, R.A. 1979: *The Python Breeding Manual*. Institute for Herpetological Research.

Spawls, S. 1989: "Some Notes and Reminiscences on the Royal Python, *Python regius* in Ghana and elsewhere." *Snake Keeper*, Vol. 3, No. 3, pp. 11–14.

Captive Reproduction
of Ball Pythons

By Tracy Barker and David Barker

B all pythons can be reproduced successfully in captivity with considerable predictability. Many hobbyists have successfully bred their captive ball pythons, although these breedings have seldom received much notice. To date, the most prominent success in breeding this species has been with albino ball pythons. Numerous python keepers are now working with these animals, and their endeavors to establish a strain of albino ball pythons in herpetoculture have resulted in three generations of ball pythons in captivity.

Sex Determination

Both sexes of ball pythons have large cloacal spurs. The spurs of older adult male ball pythons are often worn, their tips blunt and rounded, and sometimes they appear smaller than the spurs of a similar-size female; however, in adult specimens, the spurs of males, when intact, are larger and have a more inward hook than the spurs of females.

Adult ball pythons are best sexed by introducing a smooth, blunt, slender, and lubricated probe into the cloaca; by pushing the probe against the posterior wall of the cloaca, one can determine if it can be freely but gently pushed into the base of the tail. The probe can be deeply inserted into the base of the tail of males, passing inside the inverted hemipenis. The sexes can be distinguished by the probe passing deeper into the base of the tail of a male than into that of a female. A sexing probe will pass into the tail of a male ball python a distance spanning eight to ten subcaudal scales, while it typically can be inserted only a distance of two to four subcaudals in female snakes.

Ball pythons of any age can be sexed by probing the cloaca for the presence of hemipenes, but hatchlings can be easily sexed using a method known as "popping." To perform this method, the thumb of one hand is placed on the anal scale and used to gently pull the scale

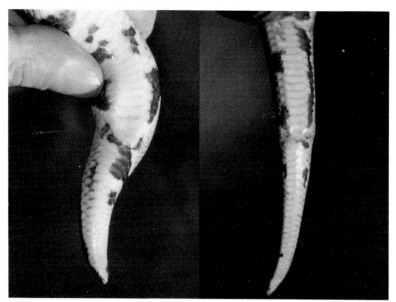

Vent areas of male (left) and female (right) ball pythons. *Photo by Chris Wood.*

Determining the sex of a ball python using a sexing probe. This specimen is a male. *Photo by Chris Wood.*

forward, exposing and slightly opening the vent. The thumb of the other hand is placed on the subcaudal surface of the base of the tail and, applying gentle pressure with a rocking motion toward the vent, attempts to evert the hemipenes of males. The hemipenes of hatchling males are small and have a visible red blood vessel on their medial surface.

Ball pythons can be sexed with certainty using the "popping" method *only* during the first few weeks after hatching. After that time the young males gain sufficient muscle control of their hemipenes to render sex identification uncertain. Hatchling ball pythons are delicate, so it is critical to their physical well-being to restrain them gently when they are being sexed, and to avoid subjecting their spine to excessive compression or stretching.

Sexual Maturity

In order to breed, ball pythons must be old enough and large enough, but these two factors are variable. As is important in the breeding of any animal, overall health, condition, and weight are major considerations. Reproduction is taxing and metabolically expensive for female ball pythons. The responsible breeder must carefully assess the condition of his or her animals, making the decision to breed them only if their overall physical condition is excellent.

Male ball pythons likely produce viable sperm by six months of age, but they should not be expected to be sexually active at that time. Males become predictably reproductively active at a weight of about 650 grams, usually at 16 to 18 months of age. Even so, young males may be tentative in their breeding attempts; older males, animals exceeding three years of age and 1,000 grams in weight, tend to be the best breeders.

Females usually must exceed 1,000 grams in weight to reproduce successfully. The first potential breeding season for most females is their third winter; at that time most females are 27 to 31 months of age. There are records of ball python females producing fertile eggs after mating during their second winter, but this is rare and the few resulting clutches for which we have records are small, numbering between one and four eggs.

Weight Gain in Female Ball Pythons

weight in grams

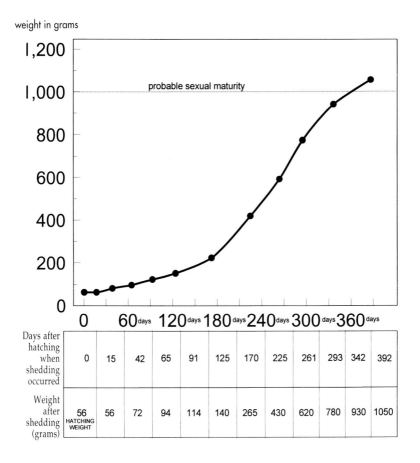

Days after hatching when shedding occurred	0	15	42	65	91	125	170	225	261	293	342	392
Weight after shedding (grams)	56 HATCHING WEIGHT	56	72	94	114	140	265	430	620	780	930	1050

This graph is based on the average of the data recorded for three captive-bred female ball pythons. These animals were kept in optimum conditions, as evidenced by their rapid growth. The animals were weighed and the weight recorded after each shedding.

Reproductive Longevity

Ball pythons have long reproductive lives and can reproduce through their twenties. A female ball python housed at the St. Louis Zoo for 32 years laid a clutch of fertile eggs when she was estimated to be 35 years of age.

Natural Reproductive Cycles

Ball pythons are nearly equatorial in distribution; most of the range of the species is found between 5 and 15 degrees north latitude. There is little variation in day length near the equator, and natural light cycles approximate 12 hours of light and 12 hours of dark throughout the year. Daily temperatures typically vary from 90 to 110° F (32.2 to 43° C) during the warmest time of the year, and from 75 to 86° F (25 to 31° C) during the cool periods of the year.

Ball pythons in nature are seasonal breeders. The natural reproductive cycle in Ghana and Togo (the geographic origin of most ball pythons in captivity) appears to be correlated with the two cool rainy periods expected in years of normal weather. Mating pairs of ball pythons are most commonly encountered from mid-September through mid-November. This period of time is known as the minor rainy season, a relatively cool couple of months during which it rains almost every day. The dry season begins at the end of November, and the weather becomes progressively hotter and drier through March, the hottest month. Most ball python eggs are laid during the last half of the dry season, from mid-February to the beginning of April. The major rainy season usually begins in mid-April with several weeks of intermittent showers; April and May are hot and steamy, June and July begin to cool, the rains end in mid-July, and August typically is dry and is the coolest month of the year. Most ball python eggs hatch during the period from mid-April to mid-June.

Captive Reproduction

Kept at constant temperatures and day lengths throughout the year, captive ball pythons seldom produce fertile eggs, even though they may mate. In captivity, ball pythons usually require the manipulation of environmental conditions to trigger successful reproduction.

It is not necessary to reproduce exactly the annual climatic patterns of West Africa in order to reproduce captive ball pythons; in fact, we are not aware of its ever being attempted. Breeders of ball pythons typically provide a gradually changing annual light cycle varying from 15 hours of light at summer solstice to 9 hours of light at winter solstice.

We feed ball pythons weekly through the fall in preparation for their winter fast. Many male ball pythons and some female ball pythons cease feeding at some point during the fall, as the days become shorter. For those animals that have continued to feed, feeding is stopped during the last week of November. Beginning in mid-December we lower the ambient temperatures to usual daytime maximums of 82° F (28° C) and nighttime minimums of 75° F(24° C). We maintain these winter ambient temperatures until the last week of February, at which time we resume the normal maintenance temperatures. We offer ball pythons food after this cool period, usually during the first week of March. We have occasionally observed ball

A "striped" ball python hatched by Philippe de Vosjoli. The eggs in the clutch were incubated at fluctuating temperatures.

pythons to experience minimum temperatures as low as 61° F (16° C) for overnight periods without apparent ill effects.

During the winter cooling period, we provide each ball python with a supplemental basking spot providing a small area of warm temperatures of 85-90° F (29-32° C). Typically we observe males and females both spending little time basking during December and January. In February we have observed them to begin spending increasing amounts of time in these warm spots, usually basking several hours daily.

In late February, when the winter cooling period is discontinued, we continue to provide ball pythons with a basking spot, increasing the temperature and providing daily fluctuation of temperatures at the basking spot from nighttime lows of 86° F (30° C) to daytime highs of 95° F (35° C).

Usually, male ball pythons will live together amicably, but occasionally during the winter we have observed male ball pythons introduced together to combat. In general the combat is harmless, consisting of much pushing and wrestling. The objective of each participant appears to be either to raise its head over the head of the other, or to push the head of the other to the ground with its body. Although we

Female ball python brooding a clutch of eggs. *Photo by Philippe de Vosjoli.*

have not observed biting to be a component of ball python combat, we have commonly seen it in other python species; thus, it is a good idea to watch combatting ball pythons to make certain that none of the participants resort to biting. When biting occurs as a part of male combat of other species of pythons, trauma can result, including deep wounds, eye injuries, skin tears, and (although rarely) the death of one of the combatants.

Combat often will stimulate inactive male pythons to court and breed with females that are placed in their cages. Many python breeders purposely place males together, encouraging combat between them, before placing the males with females for mating.

We place male and female ball pythons together in late December. A male may be placed with up to five females. In some cases the pairs or groups remain together until late March, but pairs may be introduced together weekly for three-day periods and then separated and returned to their own cages. We most often place females in the cages of males, but placing males into the cages of females seems to work equally well.

We observe two general periods of copulation, usually during the shortest day lengths and coolest temperatures in January, and again in March after the females have resumed feeding. Females typically ovulate during the period of mid-March through April, from 6 to 30 days after the last observed copulation.

The time of ovulation is clearly marked by a sudden large mid-body swelling. This swelling is created by the synchronous release by both ovaries of all follicles. Once released from the ovaries, the follicles are termed *ova*, and the ova are pushed forward in the body cavity to the opening of each of the two oviducts, which lie anterior to the ovaries near the halfway point of the ball python's length. The ova are pushed forward, jammed together at the oviducts' openings by the muscular compression and tight coils of the body posterior to the swelling. Following ovulation and the mid-body swelling, the ova are taken into the oviduct and then passed posteriorly through the oviduct. The mid-body swelling diminishes as all the ova are positioned along the lengths of the oviducts where they are shelled, and the snake resumes relatively normal proportions and symmetry. The mid-body swelling in ball pythons lasts about 24 hours and is most apparent and exaggerated for about eight hours in the middle of that period.

Usually 20 days after ovulation, a female ball python begins a shed cycle. During this period of time many females will continue to eat; others will cease feeding after ovulation. Eggs are laid between 24 and 34 days (average 28.4, n=16) after shedding their skin. We have not observed females to eat during the period between the shed and egg laying; we recommend that during this four-week period gravid females *not* be offered food.

Egg laying usually occurs at night; females are typically discovered coiled around their eggs in the morning. If allowed, females will coil around their clutches until hatching. We have not observed muscular twitching or shivering in brooding female ball pythons, or other evidence that this species is able to raise its body temperature metabolically while brooding, as we have observed in several other python species. Brooding female ball pythons sometimes temporarily leave their clutch to bask, and they have been known to drink and feed during these brief periods away from their eggs.

Reproductive Effort

A clutch of ball python eggs commonly represents a significant percentage of the female's weight, ranging from 16.8 to 64.9 percent. The average ratio in 18 clutches was 46.7 percent.

Eggs

Ball python eggs measure 71–96 mm in length (averaging 84.3 mm, n=20 eggs), 46–55 mm in diameter (averaging 49.5 mm, n=20 eggs), and 65–103 g in weight (averaging 86 g, n=160 eggs). We have records of clutches of fertile eggs varying in size from 1 to 11 eggs, with an average number of 6.5 fertile eggs per clutch (n=22 clutches). The eggs are large and white or off-white in color and typically are adhered together. We incubate ball python eggs at 90 °F, and the eggs hatch in 53 to 60 days, averaging 57 days (n=22 clutches).

Ball python eggs can easily be "candled" to check for fertility. In a darkened room place a small flashlight against an egg, illuminating the inside of the egg. Fertile eggs are lighted with an overall pinkish glow, and you can see small thin red blood vessels on the inside of the shell. Infertile eggs typically are lighted with a yellow glow, and no blood vessels are apparent.

The general maintenance and environmental requirements of ball python eggs is the same as for eggs of large python species. In order to hatch, ball python eggs require high relative humidity, but not wet or damp conditions. We recommend temperatures of 86 91° F (30–32.8° C) to successfully incubate ball python eggs.

Females can be allowed to brood the eggs until hatching in conditions of high humidity and cage temperatures of 86–88° F (30–31.1° C). It is critical that the eggs be on a dry surface.

We remove the eggs from the females and incubate them in slightly damp vermiculite at 90° F. We use 13-gallon plastic trash cans as egg containers, covering each top with a pane of glass. We place 8 to 10 gallons of vermiculite in these egg containers, adding just enough water so that, once mixed, the vermiculite will just clump if squeezed in the hand. We then place the egg container in a room that is heated and thermostatically regulated to maintain a constant 90° F. An alternative is to use large plastic storage containers (such as those made by Rubbermaid®), which can be placed inside an incubator. Do not overcrowd eggs—they should cover no more than 50 percent of the vermiculite surface.

Ball python eggs are fairly hardy and you can gently handle and examine an egg or a clutch without negative effects. We think that the best way to determine if the eggs are in the proper humid conditions is to weigh them. In "dry" conditions, python eggs lose weight; in "wet" conditions, they gain weight. We have seen python eggs hatch with weights before hatching that varied from the weights at laying by minus 20 percent to plus 100 percent. At either of those extremes, however, there is a high percentage of mortality. Ball python eggs seem to fare best with a weight gain of 10 to 40 percent during incubation.

Ball python eggs usually dimple about two weeks before hatching. During the last week of incubation, the egg shells become increasingly thin and pliable. Three or four days before hatching, the eggs in a clutch begin to lose their adhesion to each other, and the eggs in the clutch can be easily separated.

When hatching, a baby ball python slits several openings in the shell with its egg tooth, and then pokes its head out of the egg. At this time a hatching ball python usually has a large amount of yolk outside its body and is still connected to its umbilicus by large blood vessels. This yolk is being quickly absorbed into its body, after which time its umbilicus will close. The hatching ball python usually will not leave the egg until this process is completed, a period of 24 to 36 hours after it slits the egg. As soon as hatchlings emerge from the shell, they should be transferred to a clean enclosure with adequate heat, a shelter, water, and relatively high ambient humidity.

Breeders often house captive-hatched ball pythons individually in plastic shoe boxes containing a small water dish. The box is placed on a shelf with heat tape on a rheostat running along one side. This housing method works for short-term keeping of large numbers of animals. A shoe box is small enough that it coincidentally provides some of the features of a shelter, particularly if the top is solid or when the box is placed between two wooden shelves.

Recognition and Treatment of Diseases and Disorders in Ball Pythons

By Roger J. Klingenberg, DVM

Captive Stress Syndrome and Immune System Support

Wild-caught and imported ball pythons are more dramatically affected by the stresses of captivity than are most other wild imports. These secretive and gentle snakes appear to be overwhelmed by captive conditions in which other reptiles readily flourish. Among other effects, the stress of captivity alters their hormonal secretions, which affect many of their day-to-day physiological functions and behavior.[1] Of the affected physiological processes, perhaps the most important is the suppression of the immune system. Current veterinary knowledge places great emphasis on supporting the immune system of these reptiles, both to prevent medical problems and to augment treatment when they do arise.[2]

Providing Heat

The easiest and most important way to support the immune system of a ball python is to provide a thermal gradient that reaches the upper preferred optimal temperature zone. Numerous studies have demonstrated that reptiles with access to such thermal gradients produce a better-coordinated immune response—including better antibody production,[3] better cellular mobilization,[4] and better suppression of pathogens—in that reptiles create a "behavioral fever" by selecting warm areas when they are ill.[5] The performance of certain antibiotics (for example, Amikacin) administered at these higher temperatures was improved because of better drug distribution and lower bacterial resistance.[6] The safety of these antibiotics was also improved because of a more rapid and efficient elimination from the body at higher temperatures.[6]

Ambient daytime temperatures of 78 to 86° F (25 to 29° C), with a nighttime drop to no lower than 73° F (22.8° C) are appropriate for the ball python. Ideally, a basking site reaching temperatures of 90 to 95° F (32 to 35° C) should be provided for several hours each day. This basking site can be provided either by an overhead light or by an undertank heating pad. Sick ball pythons are typically maintained at the upper end of these temperature ranges, but a gradient allowing them to avoid heat stress is also important.

Correcting Dehydration

The second most important means of supporting the immune system of ball pythons is to provide adequate hydration. Sick ball pythons are usually dehydrated as a result of shifts of fluids and electrolytes in the body; merely providing a water dish is unlikely to correct these deficits. You can recognize a dehydrated snake by its loss of skin elasticity, which appears as wrinkles running laterally down the body (see *Fig. 1*). In more advanced cases of dehydration, the eyes have a sunken appearance. A simple way to correct dehydration is to administer Gatorade® (The Gatorade Co., Chicago, Ill.) or Pedialite® (Ross Labs, Columbus, Ohio) by means of a gastric tube. Both liquids offer easily absorbed fluids, electrolytes, amino acids, and sugars. The author prefers to use Sovereign red rubber tubes

Fig 1. Dehydrated ball python. This ball python is clinically dehydrated, as evidenced by the lateral folds of the skin. As is often the case, this snake is also malnourished and parasitized. *Photo by Roger Klingenberg.*

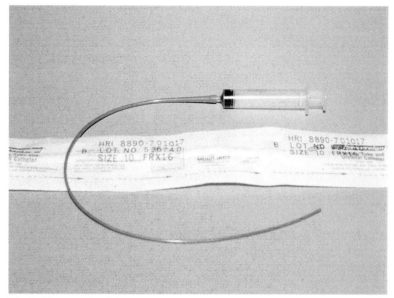

Fig 2. These red rubber tubes are trimmed at their flared ends so as to adapt to the tip of a syringe. These tubes are soft and atraumatic, yet rigid enough to allow passage. *Photo by Roger Klingenberg.*

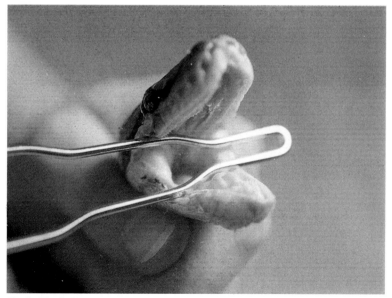

Fig 3. The ball python's mouth is opened to expose all internal structures and to allow the passage of a red rubber tube. In this case an avian speculum is used to keep the mouth open. *Photo by Roger Klingenberg.*

Fig 4. A ball point pen or long-handled cotton swab can also be used to open the mouth. It is important to use a gag that is minimally traumatic to the teeth and oral tissues. The mouth is teased open; excessive force is to be avoided. *Photo by Roger Klingenberg.*

Fig 5. The red rubber tube is introduced through the center of the speculum and advanced against the roof of the mouth and down into the oesophagus. Lubricating the tube with water or a small amount of alimentary diet (a/d) allows for an easier passage. *Photo by Roger Klingenberg.*

Fig 6. The tube is advanced until only a few inches remain. The syringe containing the feeding formula is attached to the trimmed end of the catheter and the mixture administered slowly but steadily over the course of a minute. If reflux of the mixture is seen, then immediately remove the catheter and the gag and allow the snake to swallow. Avoid excessive handling for 24 to 48 hours after feeding. *Photo by Roger Klingenberg.*

(Sherwood Medical, St. Louis, Mo.) whose ends have been cut to adapt to a syringe (see *Fig. 2*). The fluids should be administered at the rate of 10–20 ml per kg (of body weight of the snake) every 24–48 hrs. as needed.[7] This method is illustrated in *Fig. 3–6*. Dehydration should be corrected before you address nutritional needs.

Nutritional Supplementation

Very thin, ill ball pythons that are not feeding require nutritional supplementation. The author uses alimentary diet (a/d) (Hills Prescription Diets) or a homemade force-feed mix (instructions follow). Hills a/d is a chicken-based syringeable food, available from veterinarians, that provides an ideal combination of nutrients, vitamins, minerals, and electrolytes to prevent further tissue wasting[2]. The a/d is fed at a rate of one ounce (30 ml) per kg every 7–21 days, as needed. Mildly dehydrated snakes can have the a/d mixed at a one-to-one ratio with Lactated Ringers solution, Gatorade®, or Pedialite®. Very emaciated animals should be fed every 7–10 days initially, and

The proper way to inject a ball python. Because snakes have a renal portal system, they should be injected in the anterior (front) third of their bodies. *Photo by Roger Klingenberg.*

every 21 days when their condition is stable. Although a ball python could be nutritionally maintained in this manner, the goal is to sustain the animal only until it is sufficiently adapted to captivity or well enough to start feeding on its own. Many experienced herpetoculturists refuse to force-feed a ball python, for fear of causing it even more stress. This author does agree that ball pythons with good body mass and no serious ailments need *not* be force-fed. It is vital, however, for an emaciated and ill ball python to receive basic sustenance.

HOMEMADE FORCE-FEED MIX

1 jar puréed chicken baby food
1 jar Gatorade® or Pedialite®
1/4 teaspoon vegetable oil
1 Tums® tablet, crushed (provides calcium)

Mix all ingredients well and feed at the same rate as the a/d:
one oz (30 ml) per kg every 7–21 days, as needed.

By supporting the immune system with an appropriate temperature gradient, correcting dehydration, and providing nutritional supplementation, the following disorders and diseases are much easier to manage.

Ball Python Health Trouble-Shooting Chart—I

Anatomical Region	Symptom	Most Common Cause	Treatment
Head			
Eyes	Opaque, film on eye(s)	Retained eye cap	Increase humidity by light misting. Apply artificial tears ointment by eyes twice daily until loosened. Do not force loosening unnecessarily.
	Eye enlarged and bulging	Infected eye, glaucoma, trauma	See veterinarian as this ailment requires professional diagnosis and likely will need topical and systemic medications.
	Rim of eye elevated, puffy appearance	Mite infestation of postorbital space	Applying artificial tear ointment daily will suffocate mites. A small sexing probe can be gently moved around the postorbital space to mechanically eliminate the mites. General mite treatment is also recommended.
Nostrils	Occluded (plugged), with open-mouth breathing	Retained shed, dried secretions from respiratory infections	For retained shed, apply artificial tear ointment (as with retained eye cap) until loosened and then mechanically remove. Observe for signs of respiratory disease.
Mouth	Mild distortion, hemorrhage spots, viscous secretions or cheeselike pus, excess salivation	Infectious stomatitis (mouth rot) or infected tooth	Increase heat. Gentle surgical removal of loose tissues with nolvasan, betadine, or peroxide. In all but the mildest cases, see veterinarian for systemic antibiotics. In case of infected teeth, simply pull tooth and clean mouth with aforementioned disinfectants. If problem doesn't resolve quickly, see veterinarian.

Ball Python Health Trouble-Shooting Chart—II

Anatomical Region	Symptom	Most Common Cause	Treatment
Throat	Distended, inflated; appears to bulge underneath	Usually associated with respiratory infections	Increase heat. Make sure animal is not in respiratory distress. In all but the mildest cases, see veterinarian.
Respiratory			
Glottis and Trachea	Frothy saliva, open-mouth breathing, head elevated, clicking, popping, or wheezing noises	Respiratory infection	Increase heat. Make sure animal is not in respiratory distress. In all but the mildest cases, see veterinarian for antibiotics and drying agents. Occasionally will need nebulization.
Neurological			
Attitude, Posture, Behavior	Inappropriate tongue flicking, jerky movements, lying on side or back, "gazing"	Meningitis, encephalitis; sometimes called "star gazing;" also caused by heat, viruses, tumors, trauma, and (rarely) by amoebic protozoans	Occasionally caused by overheating, usually in excess of 100° F for more than a few hours. Almost all cases caused by bacterial infection. See veterinarian for diagnostic information and typical systemic antibiotic and steroid anti-inflammatory therapy. Flagyl (metronidazole) is used successfully in some cases for its antibacterial activity.
Skin			
	Excess dried skin, with edges that are peeled up but will not come off	Retained shed	Increase humidity by misting frequently. If resistant, soak in 10-gallon aquarium with moistened bath towels and a loose cover to maintain high humidity. Short-duration soaks may only leave skin drier.

Ball Python Health Trouble-Shooting Chart—III

Anatomical Region	Symptom	Most Common Cause	Treatment
Skin (continued)	Defined areas of dry, shrunken scales	Bacterial dermatitis, usually mistaken for fungus; also look for localized areas of mites	Use a newspaper substrate while treating. Apply anti-biotic ointment (neosporin, polysporin, etc.) once daily for 2–3 weeks. Use betadine ointment if fungus is suspected. If nonresponsive, see veterinarian.
	Scales with reddish color on belly, brown crumpled scales, ulcerated areas	Necrotic dermatitis (scale rot)	Increase temperature. Use newspaper for substrate. Apply antibiotic ointment as with bacterial derma-titis. In all but the mildest cases, see veterinarian.
	Elevated scales with small protruberances	Ticks	Pull ticks by firmly grasping with tweezers and pulling. Apply antibiotic ointment once daily for 7 days. If infected, see veterinarian. Continue to observe for more ticks.
	Soft, fluctuant masses	Aberant, migrating tapeworms	Lance area between scales (1/8 in.) and tease out with a needle or grasp with tweezers. Flush area with nolvasan, betadine, or peroxide and apply antibiotic ointment once daily for 5–7 days. Treat snake for tapeworms.
	Firm skin masses	Abcesses, cysts, granulomas, tumors	See veterinarian for diagnosis and treatment plan. Needle biopsy is easy diagnostic tool.
Body	Not gaining weight despite eating well	Parasitism	Have fecal sample analyzed or parasite passed exam-ined. If parasites are present, treat with products and doses suggested in following section on parasitism.

Ball Python Health Trouble-Shooting Chart—IV

Anatomical Region	Symptom	Most Common Cause	Treatment
Body (continued)	Rear third of body distended; also, not eating	If female, likely gravid. If male, suspect severe constipation with possible intestine rupture	Set up cage conducive to egg laying. See chapter on breeding and reproduction. For suspected constipation, see section below and/or consult veterinarian.
	Firm mass(es) within the body	Uric acid balls, retained fecal masses, or retained eggs	If you suspect uric acid stones or fecal masses, try soaking the snake in tepid water to encourage defecation. If this produces no results or source is unknown, see veterinarian for possible x-ray.
Gastrointestinal			
	Bloody, mucus-laden, or very rancid feces	Parasitism or gastro-enteritis (usually bacterial)	Have fecal evaluation performed. If no parasites are seen, a fecal culture and antibiotic may be needed.
	Regurgitation	Gastroenteritis: parasites, protozoans, bacteria, inadequate heat for digestion; also, foreign bodies	Withhold food for a few days; make sure the snake is well hydrated and warm. Resume feedings, small food items given infrequently. Palpate for foreign bodies (retained skulls, uric acid balls masses, etc.). If no other findings, consider having appropriate cultures and exam done by veterinarian. One dose of Flagyl at 25–40 mg/kg will often clear mild bacterial and protozoal cases. Do not handle for at least 48 hours after feeding.

Disorders with Special Emphasis in Ball Pythons

Parasitism

Although parasites are fairly uncommon in captive-born ball pythons, they are the rule rather than the exception in wild-caught imports. At one time in the author's veterinary practice 300 consecutive ball pythons examined had at least one internal parasite, and most of them had multiple parasites[8]. Fecal testing performed on several hundred ball pythons leads the author to estimate that more than 95 percent of wild-caught specimens harbor internal parasites, and that close to 40 percent host external parasites (primarily ticks).

It is imperative that these parasites be eliminated if your ball pythons are to prosper. The following drugs and doses proved to be very safe and effective in the treatment of the several hundred ball pythons previously mentioned.

Fenbendazole (Panacur®, Hoechst-Roussel) dosed at 25 mg per kg orally once every 7–10 days for at least three treatments will eliminate nematode parasites (roundworms, hookworms, etc.)[8,9]. Ivermectin (Ivomec®, Merck), while also effective against nematode parasites, is not used by the author for ball pythons because of the chance of rare neurological effects.[8,9] Praziquantel (Droncit®, Mobay) dosed at 5–8 mg per kg, either orally or injected, is effective against cestodes (tapeworms) and some trematodes (flukes)[9]. Sulfadimethoxine (Albon®, Roche) is effective for coccidia when dosed at 50 mg per kg orally once daily for three days, off three days, then repeated for three more days.[9] Flagellates can be treated with Metronidazole (Flagyl®, Searle) at doses ranging from 25 to 40 mg per kg orally, and repeated in three days if needed.[9]

Ticks are removed with tweezers and the wound treated with a topical antibiotic ointment daily for a week. As ticks can transmit bacterial diseases while feeding on the host, systemic antibiotics are often indicated.

Mites can be treated in individual ball pythons with No-pest strips (impregnated with 2.2 dichlorovinyl dimethyl phosphate), Ivomec® spray, or pyrethroid sprays[9]. For individual cases, a small piece of No-pest strip inside a jar with holes punched in the lid can be placed in the cage for three to four hours, two to three times weekly for three weeks. In larger collections, a dilute Ivermectin spray (10 mg or 1cc of 1% Ivomec® to one quart water) is sprayed liberally in the cage and on the animal every 4–5 days as needed. Although the author doesn't use Ivermectin for internal nematode parasites, this concentration of Ivermectin has not caused any problems to date. In both methods the water dish must be removed while the pest strip is present and until the spray is dry. No- pest strips should be used *only* in cages with good ventilation. The author has recently had the best results using the Ivermectin spray on the animal and in the cage, and using a pyrethroid-based spray with residual action outside the cage and on shelves. The Ivermectin spray can also be used outside the cage and on shelves, but the length of its duration is unknown. Thorough cage cleaning and the elimination of noncleanable hiding materials are essential for any of these methods to work.

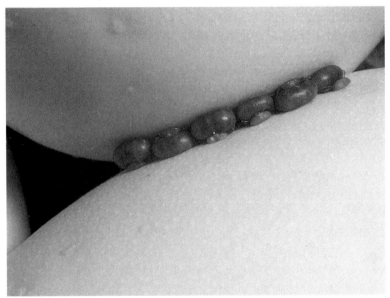

One species of tick is common in imported ball pythons; its life cycle is somehow tied to the life cycle of these snakes. Following egg-laying, paired ticks will migrate from the female ball python to the eggs. *Photo by David Barker.*

Skin Infections

Ball pythons tend to have a high incidence of skin problems, which are often related to external parasites. Necrotizing dermatitis or "scale rot" is common, as well, and signs of infection should be aggressively treated. The earliest sign of infection is bleeding into the belly scales, which appears as a red to pinkish tint to the scales. While this is a normal pigment change in some snakes (boa constrictors, for example), it is *not* normal in the ball python.

Provide your snake with a water dish that is just large enough to drink from but not large enough to soak in. Some ball pythons use large dishes to hide in, and consequently they get waterlogged. Excessive soaking may also indicate the presence of mites, so you should search for dead mites in the bottoms of such dishes.

Excessive moisture can predispose the snakes to skin problems, but external parasites and the local manifestation of a severe septicemia are more commonly involved. The skin appears to be a weak organ system in ball pythons and is affected by many common disorders.

Gastrointestinal Disorders

A common complaint in newly acquired captive imports is regurgitation and/or the production of copious mucus-laden, blood-tinged, or excessively fetid stools. Gastroenteritis, an inflammation of the gastrointestinal lining, is generally caused by internal parasites, protozoans, bacterial infections, and/or poor husbandry techniques. Internal parasites and protozoans are discovered by fecal examination and treated with appropriate medications. Inadequate heat can cause immune suppression and prevent the normal digestion of foodstuffs in the gastrointestinal tract. Excessive handling within two to three days of feeding may cause regurgitation in nervous ball pythons.

Bacterial infections are common, perhaps because opportunistic bacteria take advantage of a weakened host. The maintenance of normal intestinal bacterial flora is dependent on regular feeding and elimination. Most imported ball pythons are undernourished and dehydrated, conditions that contribute to the alteration of their normal intestinal bacterial flora, thereby allowing other bacteria to

Stomatitis (mouth rot) in a newly imported ball python. Note areas of caseous (cheesy-looking) matter. Mild infections can be treated topically, but more severe cases will require veterinary assistance. (See chart on p. 67.) *Photo by Philippe de Vosjoli.*

proliferate. These same snakes are usually exposed to dozens of other snakes, and therefore potentially to contagious parasitic, bacterial, and even some viral pathogens. For very mild cases, orally administered metronidazole (Flagyl®, Searle) at 25–40 mg per kg given as a single dose or on the first and third days may be enough to control the problem.[9] Flagyl® is used most often as an anti-protozoan drug, but it is also an excellent gastrointestinal antibiotic, especially for hard-to-detect anaerobic bacteria. In refractory cases, a fecal culture may be required to identify the causative agent and to give antibiotic choices.

When dealing with regurgitation or diarrhea, it is also important to withhold foods during treatment, in order to allow the intestinal lining to heal. Fluid therapy (as previously described) is indicated unless this also causes regurgitation. If the python appears to be doing well following treatment, initially offer only very small and infrequent meals. For a ball python weighing one kilogram, this would mean offering a pinkie rat or a very small mouse once every seven to ten days. Once the snake is eating and eliminating normally, you can gradually build up its feeding to normal amounts over the course of two to three weeks. Although it may seem difficult to overfeed a ball python, excessive feeding can create maldigestion and gastrointestinal irritation.

Reference Sources

[1] Dinardo, D.: "Stress: A Real But Not Well Understood Phenomenon." *The Vivarium*, 1993; 2 (5): pp. 25–28.

[2] Klingenberg, R.J.: "Reptile Therapeutics," *Reptile Medicine and Surgery*. Ist edition, Mader, D.R. (ed). W.B. Saunders Publishing Co. At Press.

[3] Evans, E.E.: "Comparative Immunology: Antibody Production in *Dipsosuarus dorsalis*." *Nature* 1974; 252: pp. 473–474.

[4] Kiester, Jr., E.: "A Little Fever is Good for You." *Science*, 1984: Nov. pp. 168–174.

[5] Kluger, M.J.: "Fever in ectotherms: evolutionary implications." *American Zool*. 1979;19: pp. 295–304.

[6] Mader, D.R., G.M. Conzelman, and J.D. Baggot: "Effects of Ambient Temperature on the Half-life and Dosage Regimen of Amikacin in Snakes." *Journal of Veterinary Medicine*(?). 1985; 187: p. 1134.

[7] Klingenberg, R.J.: "Anorexia in Reptiles." *Proceedings of the Twelfth International Symposium on Captive Propagation and Husbandry in Reptiles*. New York-New Jersey, June 15–18, 1988: pp. 109–122.

[8] Klingenberg, R.J.: "A Comparison of Fenbendazole and Ivermectin for the Treatment ofNematode Parasites in Ball Pythons." *The Bulletin of the Association of Reptile and Amphibian Veterinarians*. Vol. 2, No. 2, pp. 5–6.

[9] Klingenberg, R.J.: "Understanding Reptile Parasites." 1st edition. Advanced Vivarium Systems, Lakeside, Ca., 1993.

Index

NOTES